AF594039

LED ZEPPELIN

LED ZEPPELIN

William Ruhlmann

LONGMEADOW
PRESS

Page 1: ***Led Zeppelin displaying a range of footwear during a photo session in France.***

Page 2: ***The band on stage in the early days.***

This page: ***A moody publicity shot for Atlantic Records.***

For Margie.
Special thanks to Jeff Tamarkin for his help.

This 1992 edition published by
Longmeadow Press
201 High Ridge Road
Stamford CT 06904

Produced by
Brompton Books Corporation
15 Sherwood Place
Greenwich CT 06830

ISBN 0-681-41679-3

Printed in Hong Kong

0 9 8 7 6 5 4 3 2 1

Contents

CHAPTER ONE

Introducing The Band

On July 23, 1985, an audience of 20,000 at New Jersey's Brendan Byrne Arena was applauding the end of a performance by ex-Led Zeppelin lead singer Robert Plant, when he gave them something more to cheer about: for the encore, he brought out his former partner, Jimmy Page. Though Plant had launched his solo career three years before and already had one platinum and two gold albums to show for it, a look around his audience indicated that no one had forgotten his old band: everywhere, fans sported T-shirts and badges reading 'Led Zeppelin.'

Naturally, Page's appearance set off an ecstatic roar, and only when it had subsided slightly could Plant be heard. 'Is there anything you'd like to hear?' he asked playfully. As one voice, 20,000 people shouted back, 'Stairway To Heaven!' The band launched into an unidentified blues instead, but the crowd was grateful for what it had received. Led Zeppelin lived again.

If such a demonstration indicated that, almost five years after its demise, Led Zeppelin remained as important to rock fans as ever, another seven years have done nothing to diminish that importance. Popularity is what the music business is all about, but it's hard to think of many performers who could, with a single announcement, sell out as many stadiums in the US as they might desire. In 1989, The Who and the Rolling Stones demonstrated they could. Certainly, Bruce Springsteen retains that kind of commercial potency, as does U2. It's possible a Police reunion could play to sold-out stadiums. And of course, if the surviving Beatles got together . . . but that's about it. These few and, of course, Led Zeppelin.

Commercial acceptance has been a constant in the band's history practically from the start. In the 12 years, 1968–1980, that Led Zeppelin existed, they were arguably one of the most popular acts in the music business forming a powerful pact with their audience.

A part of this may be due to the accident of when the band first appeared, and the ways in which its unusual career strategies worked for it. Appropriately, Led Zeppelin found its initial fame in 1969, the year of Woodstock. It was with Woodstock that rock revealed itself as a mass movement, capable of attracting legions of followers in a way that no previous form of popular music had done, and Zeppelin was a band perfectly suited to take advantage of this.

Though it played a few small gigs at its start in Europe, Led Zeppelin was really a band for arenas and mass festivals. Their stage behavior, from Page's violin bow on the guitar to drummer John Bonham's flaming gong, was designed to be seen in the back rows. Its stage set, by the innovative Showco, provided the first really impressive rock lighting.

And then there was Zeppelin's music, which took rural and Chicago blues to amazing extremes of volume and feeling. It was music that demanded a response: few were neutral in their feelings about Led Zeppelin as musicians.

Ironically, in its diversity, Zeppelin was also among the hippest bands of its time. If the music of the 1960s was one largely of consensus, the end of the decade brought a fragmentation that has not yet been reversed. To a certain extent Led Zeppelin, like such predecessors as the Beatles, dabbled in a variety of musical styles, and one can hear strains of English folk music, Stevie Wonder pop, and James Brown funk along with the blues and rock 'n' roll that dominated its sound. But Zeppelin was the first really big group that sacrificed a broad appeal to a limited but passionate one. The Beatles may have been a cultural force; Led Zeppelin was a rock band.

Right: **During Led Zeppelin's mid-1970s tours, Jimmy Page frequently wore elaborately embroidered stage costumes. Here, he is seen modeling an attractive rose work design on the 1973 US tour.**

Left: ***On May 14, 1988, Led Zeppelin reunited for the closing act at Atlantic Records' 40th Anniversary concert.***

Right: ***Jimmy Page with the violin bow on the guitar that by 1973 was a regular part of the stage show.***

Below left: ***In September, 1983, Jimmy Page and other prominent British guitarists performed at benefits for ex-Faces bassist Ronnie Lane, who suffers from multiple sclerosis.***

Below: ***John Bonham augmented the standard rock drum set with tympani and a Chinese gong.***

Left: **One of Jimmy Page's most elaborate stage costumes, this one depicting Chinese dragons on the sleeves and pant legs, worn at Earl's Court in London, May, 1975. Page played a variety of guitars, but showed a decided preference for the standard Les Paul Gibson, which he wore strung much lower on his body than most guitar players do.**

Right: **Though generally less given to wearing elaborate stage costumes, Robert Plant tended to attract attention for how little he wore, and the tight fit of what he did wear. His favored outfit, as here, on the 1977 US tour, was blue jeans with a big belt buckle, rings, bracelets and necklaces, and a shirt unbuttoned to his navel. Add to that his cascade of blond hair, and you have the makings for a rock god.**

In the sixties it may have been possible to be a fan of, say, Simon and Garfunkel, the Supremes, and the Rolling Stones at the same time. But by the seventies things were much more polarized. A fan of James Taylor was unlikely to appreciate the tastes of an aficionado of the Gamble-Huff Sound of Philadelphia, and neither was likely to have much use for Led Zeppelin. Yet the market for music had expanded so much that Zeppelin could rake in amazing wealth without reaching the general pop audience at all.

In the same way that the band came along just in time to take advantage of rock's Woodstock-scale concert expansion, Led Zeppelin was also able to use the rise of FM radio and the resulting prominence of the Lp over the 45 rpm single in the late sixties to make albums its real unit measure of success. Its record label, Atlantic Records, released Led Zeppelin singles in the US (and placed six in the Top 40), but the band disavowed any interest in 45s, and in Britain Zeppelin never released a single commercially.

LED ZEPPELIN

In a reversal of record company logic, then and now, this only served to make the albums more popular. In the US, six of ten Zeppelin Lps went to number one (eight of them did in the UK). While it is not the habit of the record industry to announce specific sales figures, record companies do periodically submit information to the Recording Industry Association of America in order to have their albums certified gold (sales of at least 500,000 copies) and platinum (sales of at least a million copies). Platinum awards were introduced only in the mid-seventies, and multi-platinum awards not until the 1980s, and since Atlantic never submitted sales figures beyond initial certification, for a long time sales of Led Zeppelin's albums could only be guessed at.

But in December 1990, along with figures for its new LED ZEPPELIN boxed set, Atlantic applied for re-certification for the entire catalog. The result: Zeppelin's untitled fourth album came in at 10 million; LED ZEPPELIN II, HOUSES OF THE HOLY, and IN THROUGH THE OUT DOOR were at five million; LED ZEPPELIN (the debut album) and PHYSICAL GRAFFITI were at four million; LED ZEPPELIN III and PRESENCE were at three million; and the new LED ZEPPELIN boxed set was platinum (this indicating sales of 500,000 or more, since it was a multi-disc set).

Unmentioned by the RIAA were THE SONG REMAINS THE SAME, the film soundtrack released in 1976 that had gone double platinum by 1984, and CODA, the album of out-takes released in 1982 that had gone platinum by early the following year. Add it all up, however, and you find that Led Zeppelin has sold in excess of 43.5 million albums in the US alone since 1969. And in May 1991, when the record industry trade magazine Billboard *introduced a catalog chart to trace continuing sales of vintage albums, it became clear that Led Zeppelin's albums were still selling. The chart for the week ending June 15, 1991, for example, showed Zeppelin albums on the chart at numbers 8, 17, 24, and 33, which gave the group more listings than any other artist.*

Led Zeppelin, then, is a band that succeeded – enormously – by ignoring most of the rules by which the pop music business functions. By intention or by accident, it forged a career out of an unlikely combination of circumstances and its own musical chemistry. And 10 years after the terse announcement that terminated the band, it's obvious that Led Zeppelin can pick up, as successful as ever, any time it chooses.

Left: ***By the time of its May, 1973, US tour, Led Zeppelin was renting a Boeing 720B to fly from city to city, reflecting its status as one of the biggest touring acts in the music business. The opening night of the tour was Atlanta Braves Stadium, where the group played to 50,000 fans, a typical size for the shows on this tour.***

Above: ***Robert Plant and Jimmy Page onstage during the 1973 US tour. The tour grossed $4.5 million. It ran from May to July, concluding with three nights at Madison Square Garden in New York, during which footage was shot for what would become the film* The Song Remains the Same.**

Below: ***Led Zeppelin released only eight studio albums between 1969 and 1979. A live album was released in 1976, an album of out-takes in 1982, and a boxed set retrospective in 1990. But even with so small a catalog, Zeppelin's sales have been phenomenal, and their records continue to sell at a healthy pace to this day.***

CHAPTER TWO

Whole Lotta Love

1968-1971

Unlike many of the groups of the early sixties, which came together as the results of friendships and proximity, Led Zeppelin formed in 1968 by design. Jimmy Page (born January 9, 1944, in Heston, Middlesex), then 24 years old, already had behind him a substantial career as a studio musician that found him playing in hundreds of recording sessions. The young guitarist had benefitted from the arrival of beat music in the mid-sixties, which brought a flood of new, not-very-proficient pop stars into the studio and produced a need for session players who could recreate the new sounds. 'I had work flooding in,' he recalled later, 'as they didn't have any young guys playing guitar.' Page became a fixture on the London session scene as early as 1964, when he was 20, along with such players as keyboardist Nicky Hopkins and bassist John Baldwin (born June 3, 1946, in Sidcup, Kent), who later took the stage name John Paul Jones.

Unlike many people who enter this lucrative profession, however, Page became dissatisfied with it. 'The work was stifling,' he said. 'It was often like being a computer when you had no involvement with the artist. It should be stimulating to do sessions with other groups, but it wasn't working out that way.' Nevertheless, Page turned down the first major offer he received to join a successful rock group, and recommended that the Yardbirds, in need of a new guitarist due to the departure of Eric Clapton in February 1965, hire his friend Jeff Beck instead. They did.

But in June 1966, when bassist Paul Samwell-Smith left the Yardbirds, Page agreed to be his replacement. Soon enough, guitarist Chris Dreja had switched to bass, and the Yardbirds had two lead guitarists in Beck and Page. Beck increasingly betrayed solo aspirations, even recording a solo single, HI HO SILVER LINING/BECK'S BOLERO, in early 1967. The B-side was written and arranged by Page, and the band playing on it included the two guitarists, plus Nicky Hopkins, John Paul Jones, and drummer Keith Moon of The Who.

The Who were in danger of breaking up at the time, and Page considered forming a group, substituting The Who's John Entwistle for Jones, and perhaps adding a singer such as Steve Winwood of the Spencer Davis Group or Steve Marriott of the Small Faces. Nothing came of this plan, though it produced a usable band name. When Moon said that the band would go down like a lead balloon, Entwistle replied it would be more like a lead Zeppelin.

By the time of the release of Beck's single in March 1967, he had left the Yardbirds, who continued as a quartet. They carried on until the summer of 1968, then split, leaving Page with the group name and a set of European concert commitments. He determined to form a new group, at first to be called the New Yardbirds.

Jones had expressed an interest in being involved, and Page considered bringing in Terry Reid as lead singer, but he was unavailable. Reid, however, did have a candidate for the new group. 'He suggested I get in touch with Robert Plant, who was then in a band called Hobbstweedle,' Page said. 'When I auditioned him and heard him sing, I immediately thought there must be something wrong with him personality-wise or that he had to be impossible to work with, because I just couldn't understand why, after he told me he'd been singing for a few years already, he hadn't become a big name yet.'

Right: **Robert Plant, never seen during his Led Zeppelin days without long, curly, angelic locks parted down the middle, began as a young soul belter in England's Midlands, and even recorded a couple of unsuccessful singles during his teens. But he had joined the band with which his name would always be associated by the age of 20, and was a star before he turned 21.**

Plant (born August 20, 1948, in Bromwich, Staffs) was then 19 years old and had played in several small bands in and around Birmingham. It was remarkable, given his distinctive voice, that he hadn't been noticed yet. But then, he had avoided coming to London (though he had played the occasional gig there), and the voice was so out of the ordinary it was possible to overlook. Plant had even once been kicked out of a group by a manager who told him he couldn't sing.

Left: **Jimmy Page, around the time he joined the Yardbirds in 1966. Though only 22, Page had already spent years, and developed quite a reputation, playing guitar at recording sessions in London.**

Above: **The Yardbirds in 1966, after Page replaced Paul Samwell-Smith. From left to right: Jeff Beck, Jimmy Page, Chris Dreja, Keith Relf, and Jim McCarty.**

Right: **Jimmy Page playing the bass guitar in the Yardbirds, an instrument he didn't play for long before switching to lead guitar.**

Left: ***The Yardbirds on the TV show* Ready, Steady, Go! *in the fall of 1966, playing their latest single.***

Below left: ***During Led Zeppelin's 'Return to the Clubs' tour of England, Robert Plant sported a beard.***

Below: ***John Bonham was making £40 a week drumming for Tim Rose when Robert Plant invited him to join the New Yardbirds. It took some convincing for him to leave a steady gig like that.***

Right: ***Jeff Beck, whose 1968 edition of the Jeff Beck Group predated Zeppelin's 'heavy' sound.***

It was Plant who brought in drummer John Bonham (born May 31, 1948, Bromwich, Staffs), with whom he had worked previously, and who was now starting to work with established players such as Tim Rose. The band rehearsed in August 1968, and recorded its first album in 30 studio hours over a period of two and a half weeks. Then they toured Scandinavia as the New Yardbirds in September. (Some reports have them recording the album after the tour.)

They debuted as Led Zeppelin at Surrey University on October 15, 1968. In November, Atlantic Records in New York announced that the band, through its manager, Peter Grant (who had previously handled the Yardbirds) had been signed for one of the most lucrative deals ever given to a new group. (It was later disclosed that the amount was $200,000.) This was the first evidence that the group had deliberately set its sights on American success as its primary goal.

Led Zeppelin continued to perform dates in the UK toward the end of the year, but on December 26, the first American tour was launched in Boston. The debut album, LED ZEPPELIN, was released on January 12, 1969.

Though it showed that the band had obviously been influenced by the then current 'heavy' sound of such performers as the Jeff Beck Group (whose TRUTH album, released the previous summer, makes an interesting comparison) and labelmates the Vanilla Fudge, LED ZEPPELIN represented a new synthesis of musical styles. It mixed traditional folk blues material with more surprising, but also unacknowledged, sources (BABE

I'M GONNA LEAVE YOU was 'borrowed' from a Joan Baez album; DAZED AND CONFUSED came from folk-pop singer Jake Holmes), but the borrowings were transformed by Page's ornate, gothic guitar arrangements and Plant's amazingly penetrating tenor. Certainly, Led Zeppelin's sound would develop in later years (for one thing, Plant would start writing lyrics), but it arrived full-blown with the first album.

There is a curious kind of historical revisionism, in which it often appears as though performers who turned out to be successful and generally well-accepted critically, always enjoyed that kind of response. In the case of Led Zeppelin this is clearly not the case, though it may seem surprising today to look at some of the early critical notices. By the mid-seventies, the band had become a fact of life, and those assigned to review its records and shows tended to be fans, or at least acknowledged Zeppelin's significance in the history of rock music. But initially reactions were much more mixed.

In Britain, where there is a critical tendency to support whatever is new and British, LED ZEPPELIN was given favorable but hardly ecstatic notices, and in the US, such papers as the Los Angeles Free Press had good things to say. But Rolling

Stone, already something of a musical taste-maker, did not. John Mendelsohn, writing in the magazine's March 15, 1969, issue, admitted that Page was 'an extraordinarily proficient blues guitarist,' but also said that he was 'a very limited producer and a writer of weak, unimaginative songs.' Mendelsohn reserved his greatest enmity for Plant, however, describing him as a 'pretty soul-belter who can do a good spade imitation,' and complaining of his 'strained and unconvincing shouting.'

Above left: **Led Zeppelin, shortly after release of their first album in January, 1969, and shortly after they returned from their first US tour, where they opened for Vanilla Fudge.**

Left: **Robert Plant looking like the rural, Joni Mitchell-influenced folkie he sometimes claimed to be.**

Above: **Robert Plant and Jimmy Page onstage. Led Zeppelin, from the first, set out to conquer America, and to that end they did four tours of the US in their first year.**

Right: **Robert Plant, for once with his chest covered. In 1970 Zeppelin toured America and Europe.**

Ten years would do nothing to mellow the Rolling Stone *position. Writing in* The Rolling Stone Record Guide *(edited by Dave Marsh with John Swenson) in 1979, Billy Altman would opine, 'When Led Zeppelin's debut appeared in 1969, the anticipation built up among knowledgeable music fans, excited over the prospects of Jimmy Page (the Yardbird's last guitarist) leading his own group, was replaced by an equally king-sized disgust. Here was a band that, when not busy demolishing classic blues songs, was making a kind of music apparently designed to be enjoyable only when the listener was drugged to the point of senselessness. Page, a young veteran of the mid-sixties guitar wars, had somehow made two very important discoveries: spaced-out heavy rock drove barely pubescent kids crazy . . . And so, with virtually no critical support, Led Zeppelin was soon the biggest new band on earth.'*

Of course, Zeppelin was not in fact without any critical support, and its popular support soon became enormous. The album soared to number 10 in the US (where it would eventually spend a total of 95 weeks in the charts) and to number 6 in the UK (where it lasted 79 weeks). A single, GOOD TIMES BAD TIMES, *got to number 80 in the US.*

Following its first US tour, Zeppelin began work on a second album, then returned for a second US tour on April 20, this time as a headliner. The group was back in the UK in June, playing bigger venues, and returned for another US tour in July, when it played at the Newport Jazz Festival.

All the touring paid off in October, when LED ZEPPELIN II *was released and spent seven weeks at number 1 in the US, also topping the charts in Britain, as would the next seven Lps (a record matched only by ABBA).* WHOLE LOTTA LOVE, *issued by Atlantic in an abridged form as a single without the group's knowledge, reached number 4 in the US and went gold.*

The album simultaneously consolidated and extended the Zeppelin approach. Once again, familiar lyrics and chord progressions brought to mind the band's unacknowledged influences. Like the Rolling Stones, who issued a version of LOVE IN VAIN *around the same time, Zeppelin laid claim to the then uncopyrighted work of blues legend Robert Johnson, taking the most risqué lyrics from his* TRAVELING RIVERSIDE BLUES *('Now, you can squeeze my lemon 'til the juice run down my leg') for* THE LEMON SONG. *On the previous June 23, the group had performed a version of the original song on the 'Top Gear' BBC radio program hosted by DJ John Peel. When it was released on the* LED ZEPPELIN *box set in October 1990, the writing credit read, 'Jimmy Page & Robert Plant/Robert Johnson,' which for Zeppelin was generous.*

A living, and subsequently more incensed, songwriter was Chicago blues musician and producer Willie Dixon, the creative wellspring of Chess Records, whose 1962 composition YOU

Above left: ***John Paul Jones brought to Led Zeppelin not only his ability as a bass player, but also the talents of a keyboardist and arranger.***

Left: ***The first publicity photo of Led Zeppelin, taken in late 1968. Clockwise from the top: Jimmy Page, Robert Plant, John Paul Jones, and John Bonham.***

Above: ***Led Zeppelin looking serious in early 1969. Perhaps the photographer thought that John Bonham would become the sex symbol of the group rather than Plant.***

NEED LOVE, recorded by Muddy Waters, served as the obvious inspiration for WHOLE LOTTA LOVE. Zeppelin manager Peter Grant, in an April 1991 interview with Musician *magazine, had no trouble admitting to the group's appropriations. 'I remember a conversation one night between Jimmy Page and Mick Jagger,' he noted. 'They said, "Between us we've had the best of Chess."'*

But if one might have wished for a more honest accounting of sources at the time, a comparison of the recordings of Johnson and Waters with the songs on LED ZEPPELIN II nevertheless shows that Page had transformed them into elaborate, extended productions undreamed of by their originators. YOU NEED LOVE may serve as an outline for WHOLE LOTTA LOVE, but the remarkable arrangement that make the record the rock watershed it is, are all Page's doing.

Plant, meanwhile, had begun to contribute lyrics for the first time, and his own influences (to the extent the words could be made out) were also clear. When not belting out bad woman blues lyrics, he exhibited some of the sensitive sentiment of the emerging singer-songwriters of the day, and added to that an infatuation that would become ever more apparent for English fantasy stories and tales of knights and damsels. For example, his lines from RAMBLE ON – 'T'was in the darkest depths of Mordor / I met a girl so fair / But Golem, the evil one crept up / And slipped away with her' – referred to his readings of British fantasy novelist JRR Tolkien's THE LORD OF THE RINGS trilogy.

LED ZEPPELIN II also served as a showcase for Zeppelin's ensemble playing and individual talents. Jones, who was involved in much of the composition and arrangement of the record, remains underrated in the creation of the Zeppelin sound, and John Bonham, whose definitive drum solo, MOBY DICK, first appeared here, had begun to assert himself as a percussionist with an individuality the equal of Keith Moon or the Rolling Stones' Charlie Watts.

Like that for the first album, the critical reaction to LED ZEPPELIN II was once again mixed, with such British magazines as Melody Maker and New Musical Express praising the Lp, while the American response was more subdued. The unbowed

Left: ***Led Zeppelin has tea while preparing to do its laundry – or so it would seem. A far more tame group than their intoxicating music would suggest.***

Top: ***A more characteristic view of Robert Plant, seen here crooning in the mid-70s.***

Above: ***Only Jimmy Page declines to participate in this duel of the sullen looks.***

Right: ***'Sensitive Plant' says a sticker on the back of this photograph, taken in November, 1970, at a time when Robert Plant, recently awarded the title of Top British Male Vocalist by*** **Melody Maker*****, was starting work on Zeppelin's fourth Lp.***

Above: ***June 28, 1970. Led Zeppelin performs before 200,000 at the Bath Festival. 'The group always felt that Bath was the beginning for them in Britain,' remembered Joe Massot (co-director of*** **The Song Remains The Same*****).***

Above left: ***Jimmy Page at Bath sporting a beard.***

Left: ***Robert Plant, whose love of the English countryside and of English folklore, especially Arthurian legend, came to be reflected in Led Zeppelin's lyrics.***

John Mendelsohn, writing in Rolling Stone's *December 13, 1969 issue, responded to his own critics (one of whom had called his previous review '100% lie') with six paragraphs of unremitting sarcasm, beginning with the words, 'Hey, man, I take it all back!' 'OK –,' he wrote, 'I'll concede that until you've listened to the album eight hundred times, as I have, it seems as if it's just one especially heavy song extended over the space of two whole sides.'*

Plant, for his part, described Mendelsohn as 'just a frustrated musician,' and history has tended to be kinder to LED ZEPPELIN II *than critics of the time were.* Rolling Stone *even reneged to the extent of placing the album at number 83 in its list of the top 100 albums of the period 1967–1987, and writing, '*LED ZEPPELIN II *was like the Book of Revelation scored for an electric boogie quartet, a vision of high-decibel holocaust that combined the torrid, animalistic raunch of old Chess and Sun records with the futuristic scream of rock's latest technology pushed to the brink.'*

By the end of 1969, Led Zeppelin had no reason to worry much about critics. The band had reportedly sold $5 million worth of records in the US, where it had recently played and its second album was the fourth most successful Lp of the year (behind the cast album to HAIR, *the Beatles'* ABBEY ROAD, *and Blood, Sweat and Tears' second album).*

Zeppelin opened 1970 with a British tour, during which New Musical Express*'s Nick Logan wrote, 'It isn't hard to understand the substantial appeal of Led Zeppelin. Their current two-hour-plus act is a blitzkrieg of musically perfected hard rock that combines heavy drama with lashings of sex into a formula that can't fail to move the senses and limbs. There are few groups who could live with them on stage.' In February Zeppelin went on to Europe, and in March it returned to the US, ending the tour on April 19 in Las Vegas.*

Upon their return to the UK Page and Plant retired to a cottage called Bron-Y-Aur ('Golden Breast') in Snowdonia to write the next album. 'If we roll up somewhere with amps and

Right: ***Jimmy Page, Robert Plant, and John Bonham accept*** **Melody Maker** ***National Pop Poll Awards, September, 1970. Zeppelin unseated the Beatles as most popular group in rock music, and also took top British group, top international group, top British male vocalist, and top British album*** **(Led Zeppelin II.)**

Far right: ***John Paul Jones and Robert Plant relax backstage 1970.***

Below right: ***Led Zeppelin relaxes backstage at the Bath Festival, June 28, 1970.***

guitars, then we make electric music,' said Plant. 'But if we roll up to the farm with acoustic guitars, that's something else and that's when the acoustic stuff gets written.' Apparently, it was acoustic guitars at Bron-Y-Aur, since the material for LED ZEPPELIN III *turned out to be surprisingly low-key.*

Issued in October 1970, the album topped the US charts for four weeks, producing the Top 20 hit IMMIGRANT SONG*, but it was less successful than previous efforts. Critical notices of the time were still not favorable.* Rolling Stone *had relieved John Mendelsohn of the burden of reviewing the band, and Lester Bangs found some good things to say, though, characteristically, the compliments were backhanded when they came. For example, of* IMMIGRANT SONG *he noted, 'What's great about it, though, the Zep's special genius, is that the whole effect is so utterly two-dimensional and unreal. You could play it, as I did, while watching a pagan priestess performing the ritual dance of Ka before the flaming sacrificial altar in* FIRE MAIDENS IN OUTER SPACE *with TV sound turned off. And*

believe me, the Zep made my blood throb to those jungle rhythms even more frenziedly.'

A little less prosaically, critic Robert Christgau, who scored the album an A+ (downgraded to a B+ years later), felt that 'Plant is overpowering even when Page goes to his acoustic, as he does to great effect on several surprisingly folky (not to mention folk bluesy) cuts. No drum solos, either.' Side two of the record, wrote Billy Altman, 'represented the band's turning point . . . new directions were being formed.'

'You see,' explained Plant, 'here I am, the lead singer with Led Zeppelin, and underneath I still enjoy people like Fairport Convention and the Buffalo Springfield. Some people may find that surprising. To tell the truth, I've always wanted to go into the realm of that sort of music to a certain degree, without losing the original Zeppelin thing. Some people may have gotten the impression that I had some unfulfilled ambitions while the last two albums were getting done, but all I can say is that this album is really getting there.'

After recording the album the band had gone back on tour during the rest of 1970, playing in Iceland, the US, Britain, and Germany. The August 5 – September 19 tour of the US was Zeppelin's sixth American trip in less than two years. At the end of the year the group toured in the Far East, stopping in Australia and Japan, including a show for 6000 at Hiroshima that served as a benefit for the victims of the atomic bomb.

In March 1971, Zeppelin embarked on a tour of small ballrooms in Britain, a trek intended to show that the group wasn't only interested in high-profit tours and that it retained an interest in its homeland. The tour introduced a new, long song called STAIRWAY TO HEAVEN that Page played with a double-necked Gibson guitar, allowing him to switch from six-string playing to twelve.

When the British tour ended in April, the band retired to continue work on its fourth album, which it had begun recording in London in December 1970. This time, the bandmembers recorded at Headley Grange, their house in Hampshire,

employing the Rolling Stones' mobile recording truck. They followed the sessions with another world tour, taking in Europe, the US, and Japan.

The fourth, untitled, Led Zeppelin album was released on November 8, 1971, while the band was on tour in Britain. Although it was held out of the number 1 position in the US, the record is unquestionably Zeppelin's most popular. (In 1991, when critic Chuck Eddy published a book on the 100 best heavy metal albums of all time, he placed it at number 1.) Atlantic culled two hits, BLACK DOG (number 15) and ROCK AND ROLL (number 47) from it, although the best-known track, STAIRWAY TO HEAVEN, the most-played song on radio for the next 20 years, never appeared on a commercially issued 45.

The album also represented Zeppelin's critical breakthrough, with critic Lenny Kaye sounding the about-face in Rolling Stone: 'It might seem a bit incongruous to say that Led Zeppelin – a band never particularly known for its tendency to understate matters – has produced an album which is remarkable for its low-keyed and tasteful subtlety, but that's just the case here. . . . If this thing . . . isn't quite their best to date . . . it certainly comes off as their most consistently good.' Altman calls it 'arguably Zeppelin's finest album,' and Christgau writes, '[T]his is the definitive Led Zeppelin and hence heavy metal album. It proves that both are – or can be – very much a part of Rock and Roll.'

'To me,' said Page, 'I thought STAIRWAY crystalized the essence of the band. It had everything there and showed the band at its best . . . as a band, as a unit. Not talking about solos or anything, it had everything there. We were careful never to release it as a single. It was a milestone for us. Every musician wants to do something of lasting quality, something that will hold up for [a] long time and I guess we did it with STAIRWAY. Pete Townshend probably thought that he got it with TOMMY. I don't know whether I have the ability to come up with more. I have to do a lot of hard work before I can get anywhere near those stages of consistent, total brilliance.'

The immediate effect of the album was to catapult a group that was already enormously popular to mythic standing. Britain's Record Mirror, noting the charts for 1971, wrote, 'We must face the fact that John, Paul, George and Ringo have become, John, John Paul, Jimmy and Robert – Led Zeppelin . . . It's a phenomenon, pure and simple.'

Right: **Led Zeppelin's album output, 1969-1971. Clockwise:** Led Zeppelin, ***the untitled fourth album,*** Led Zeppelin III, ***and*** Led Zeppelin II.

Opposite page: ***John Paul Jones at the keyboard. Jones's contribution to Zeppelin, especially with regard to arrangements and keyboard work has been consistently underrated.***

Previous two pages, left: ***Robert Plant, as he typically appeared onstage in the mid-1970s, when Led Zeppelin was the most popular rock band in the world.***

Previous two pages, right: ***Jimmy Page, as he typically appeared onstage in the mid-1970s, providing a striking visual contrast in dark colors to the light-hued Plant.***

HOHNER

CHAPTER THREE

Stairway To Heaven

1972-1974

With the phenomenal success of its fourth album, Led Zeppelin, after three years in existence, had crossed from the status of most popular rock group of its brief time up to the heady level of achievement reached by only a handful of musical stars. As such, it had reached the point at which relentless touring and frequent record releases give way to long seclusion and appearances, in person and on vinyl, that are not so much regular occurrences as special events in, and of, themselves.

This became apparent as the next few years went on, but at the start of 1972 it was still business as usual. In February and March, Zeppelin toured Australia and New Zealand, attracting crowds in excess of 20,000. Again they toured the US, and returned to Japan later in the year, with European dates in the fall. A British tour began on November 30 and continued into January 1973.

Somewhere in the course of all this touring Zeppelin had recorded a fifth album, originally scheduled for release in August 1972, but pushed back because of printing problems with the cover, which depicted nude, blonde-haired children climbing a hill made up of cut stones. Such concerns with cover art (the first album, according to Grant, had cost £1800, including its cover), are indicative of the increased power of the group – Grant had cut a deal with Atlantic such that, unlike many others, Zeppelin was not charged extra for elaborate packaging – its artistic pretensions, and its position in the marketplace. Now even its album covers, designed by the Hipgnosis firm, were an important part of its image.

'We had a lot of problems with the artwork,' Plant said later of HOUSES OF THE HOLY. *'We'd taken trouble on the Lp so there didn't seem to be any reason to compromise. It was a very difficult process, because of the amount of color involved. In the end, they never got it right and it's just a piece of paper in a CD box now – so there you go. I like the album, though.'*

HOUSES OF THE HOLY *finally appeared on March 28, 1973, and spent two weeks at the top of the US charts, spawning the singles* OVER THE HILLS AND FAR AWAY *(number 51) and* D'YER MAK'ER *(number 20).*

It showed the group, undaunted by the prospect of following the massive success of the fourth album, stretching out into even more musical styles. THE CRUNGE, *a song credited to all four bandmembers, boasted a James Brown-like funk beat and featured Plant's tribute to the late R&B legend Otis Redding: 'Some other man too ain't gonna call me Mr. Pitiful / No, I don't need no respect from nobody, no.'* D'YER MAK'ER *had a reggae beat at a time when the Jamaican music was more of a rumor than an international success. And songs such as* THE OCEAN *showed the degree of rhythmic integration Jones and Bonham had achieved, while still leaving room for Page's sizzling lead runs.*

Billy Altman called the album 'a fine successor' to the fourth album, but Melody Maker*'s Chris Welch, usually a friend to the band, was cool toward it, picking out* THE CRUNGE *and* D'YER MAK'ER *for special criticism, and he would later note in his* Led Zeppelin: the Book *that the band, in particular Robert Plant, took exception to his remarks.*

Zeppelin, as usual, went back on tour, playing across Europe in March and April, and in the US (its most extensive trek yet) from May to July, opening before 49,000 at Braves Stadium in Atlanta, Georgia. On June 16, 1973, Billboard *reviewed a typical show: 'Three hours without a break, music punctuated by strobe and mirror lights, smoke floating across the stage and spinning balls of fire. Page, a master-showman, dancing about*

Right: **Robert Plant onstage at the Los Angeles Forum, March 24, 1975.**

Above left: **John Paul Jones plays bass onstage during Led Zeppelin's 10th US tour in January, 1975, a tour during which he favored shorter hair and patterned vests.**

Below left: **Led Zeppelin at the airport, June 7, 1973. Left to right: Robert Plant, Jimmy Page, John Bonham, John Paul Jones.**

Above: **Led Zeppelin's manager, Peter Grant, meets the press in New York on September 30, 1973, two months after the finish of the group's US tour, during which they were robbed of the receipts of their New York shows.**

the stage, playing guitar with violin bow or working a theremin to achieve strange sound-mixes, he never misses a note and stands out constantly. Robert possesses one of the widest vocal ranges in pop music, using echo and reverberation mikes with ease. John Paul Jones handles bass and keyboards with quiet excellence and John Bonham's drumming seems to improve constantly. A lesson in what good rock 'n' roll showmanship should be.'

The band's appearance at Madison Square Garden at the end of the tour in July was filmed for a concert movie, though it would not come out for years, and then due to unexpected circumstances.

After the tour the band took a break from concerts for the first time since its formation. It would stay off the road and out of the record stores for a year and a half. During the break, fantasy scenes were filmed for the proposed movie, and the group set up its own label, Swan Song, which eventually would release the work of Bad Company, Dave Edmunds, and others. Zeppelin also worked on a double album.

'As usual, we had more material than the required 40-odd minutes for one album,' said Page. 'We had enough material for one and a half Lps, so we figured, "Let's put out a double and use some of the material we had done previously but never released."'

Having launched the record company and completed the album, Zeppelin began its first tour of America in 18 months on January 18, 1975, playing throughout the country for two months. The album PHYSICAL GRAFFITI was released on February 24, and spent six weeks at the top of the US charts, with the single TRAMPLED UNDER FOOT getting into the Top 40.

Below: **Led Zeppelin and associates aboard their private tour jet, spring, 1973.**

Above: **John Bonham's drum solos could last half an hour or more, and end with him playing with his hands instead of his sticks.**

Right: **Robert Plant (at the LA Forum, March 24, 1975) played occasional tambourine onstage, but otherwise restricted himself to singing.**

Above left: ***The group at the Silverdome in Detroit Michigan, April 30, 1977.***

Left: ***Led Zeppelin's fifth and sixth albums,*** **Houses Of The Holy** ***(1973) and*** **Physical Graffiti** ***(1975).***

Above: ***Plant and Jones, watched by promoter Bill Graham, at Kezar Stadium, San Francisco, 1973.***

With all the time they needed in the studio, Zeppelin had constructed in PHYSICAL GRAFFITI *a sprawling, loosely structured set of rock songs, many of them mere platforms for Page's guitar excursions. It was, in a sense, the most Zeppelinish of Zeppelin albums, having none of the more accessible aspects of the fourth album's folk and early rock 'n' roll leanings. As such, it marked a separation for many fans. To this day, one can find people who, when speaking of Zeppelin, say they like only the band's early albums, while there are others for whom* PHYSICAL GRAFFITI *is Zeppelin's definitive work.*

As ever, the group continued to display its influences. KASHMIR*, inspired by a trip taken by Plant and Page through the Sahara, had a Middle Eastern feel, and, oddly, has frequently been cited in subsequent years by the bandmembers as the quintessential Zeppelin track. (How a Zeppelin track lacking a guitar solo can be considered quintessential remains a mystery.)* IN MY TIME OF DYING *was 11 minutes of blues work on a tune probably first heard by Zeppelin on Bob Dylan's first album, but in fact taken from Blind Willie Johnson's* JESUS MAKE UP MY DYING BED*. Typically, the song was credited to the four group members.*

Critical opinion was quite mixed. Rolling Stone *was favorable, although this may have been related to the band's decision to do an interview with the magazine after years of holding out.* Melody Maker *called the Lp 'pure genius,' which seems excessive, while others, praising such individual tracks as* KASHMIR*, also made the typical comment about most double albums that it was rife with fillers.*

Zeppelin returned to Britain in the spring for its first UK dates in two years, playing five shows at the 17,000-seat Earl's Court. For Led Zeppelin, which had slogged around the country playing colleges a little over six years before, a British tour now meant a multi-day stand at a single large venue near London.

In the years 1972 to 1975, then, Led Zeppelin reached and consolidated a position as the most important rock band of its time and one of the most important in rock history. Already the wealth and fame of the bandmembers had isolated them in a world of country estates and sold-out world tours in massive arenas. In a sense they never came back from that isolation, though the group's decline in the second half of its career came more due to chance than to the usual excesses that scuttled many of its peers.

Left: **John Bonham in one of his rare moments not behind a drum case.**

Below: **Jimmy Page onstage with the double-necked guitar (12-string above, 6-string below) he used to play 'Stairway To Heaven.'**

Left: **Led Zeppelin pose in Miami just prior to the start of their 1973 US tour. Clockwise from top: John Bonham, Jimmy Page, John Paul Jones, Robert Plant.**

Previous pages: **Led Zeppelin pose in February, 1977, shortly before the start of their final US tour. Left to right: Jimmy Page, John Bonham, John Paul Jones, Robert Plant.**

CHAPTER FOUR

Achilles Last Stand

1975-1980

By the mid-1970s, Great Britain had instituted a graduated income tax system that reached historically high percentages for earned income at the top end, so high, in fact, that it became more economic for people with such incomes to stay out of the country in a given year long enough to exempt themselves from being taxed as residents. Rock stars, whose yearly incomes could be very high in periods of record releases and tours, came under this category, and many British rockers became 'tax exiles' during the period, the members of Led Zeppelin among them.

Following the band's five-night tour in May 1975, therefore, the members of Led Zeppelin left Britain for a summer vacation, due to be followed by another American tour to start August 23, and then, perhaps, by a South American tour, so that Led Zeppelin wouldn't return home until the Christmas holidays.

Page and Plant traveled through northern Africa and southern Europe in June and July, then to the Greek island of Rhodes for a few days before a planned rehearsal period in Paris. Page left early, on August 3, and on the 4th, Plant, driving a rented car, hit a tree, causing injuries to himself and his wife. Plant suffered multiple fractures of the ankle and elbow, while his wife Maureen was left with a fractured pelvis and skull. The couple's two children had only minor injuries.

The tour was canceled, and Plant returned to Britain briefly for treatment, then rented a house at Malibu Beach in California, where he and Page began to write new material. With Plant unable to walk for six months, a previously unscheduled new album suddenly became the band's goal, and Jones and Bonham were in Malibu by October.

In November, Led Zeppelin's seventh album, PRESENCE, was recorded in 18 days at Musicland Studios in Munich, West Germany. Page, meanwhile, had also returned to work on Led Zeppelin's movie, filmed in 1973 and 1974, but long-since put on the shelf. At the end of 1975 he was mixing its soundtrack.

PRESENCE was released March 31, 1976, and, lacking a tour, Page and Plant did extensive interviews to promote it. 'PRESENCE was our stand against everything,' said Plant. 'Our stand against the Elements, against Chance. We were literally fighting against Existence itself. We'd left home for 12 months and it seemed that everything was about to crumble.'

Leaving aside the unusual circumstances of its composition, PRESENCE finds Led Zeppelin further into its transition to a broader, often Eastern-influenced style, less anchored in its blues roots. ACHILLES LAST STAND, the album's most prominent rocker, is an elaborate suite made up of several parts and a variety of guitar textures. While the band could also concentrate its attack in a song such as CANDY STORE ROCK, it seemed increasingly interested in exotic, ornate musical structures. The rest of the rock world might be looking to Zeppelin's first few albums as the birth of heavy metal, but by 1976 the group itself was moving on.

Critical reaction to this was mixed. Bob Meyers wrote, 'Page's songwriting has evolved into a head-on combination of electric, stylistic snatches of melody strung together with explosive, unpredictable leads. This combination makes for some disjointed song structures, but it also creates an unrelenting rawness that serves to push electric technology to a gut level. A seventies gut level sound.' But New Musical Express's Charles Shaar Murray was dismissive. 'I thought my razor was dull until I heard this album,' he wrote, adding that

Right: **A Jimmy Page solo. Page's guitar work was the bedrock of Led Zeppelin's sound.**

Left: ***Led Zeppelin in 1969, around the time of the release of*** **Led Zeppelin II.**

Right: ***John Bonham arrives at the West Coast premiere of*** **The Song Remains The Same** ***on October 21, 1976, in Los Angeles.***

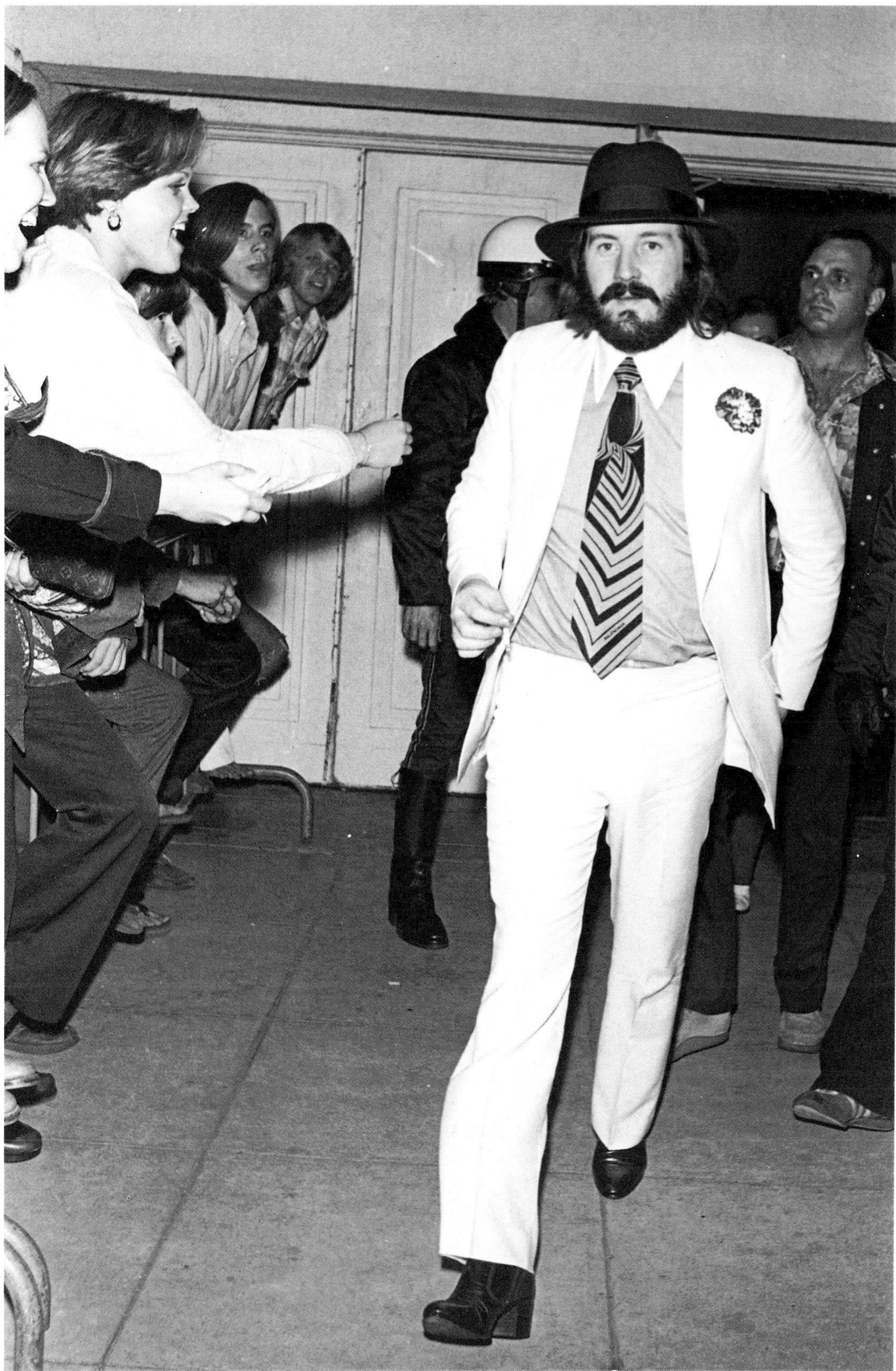

Left: ***Led Zeppelin and their manager at the West Coast premiere for*** **The Song Remains The Same,** ***October 21, 1976, Fox Theater, Los Angeles. From left to right: Peter Grant, Jimmy Page, Robert Plant, John Paul Jones, John Bonham.***

'PRESENCE never gets any higher than simply being a demonstration of capabilities and an exercise in style.' In the US, Billy Altman called PRESENCE Led Zeppelin's 'most down-to-earth album,' though Robert Christgau was unforgiving. 'Originals and influentials they obviously are,' he acknowledged, 'but too often individual pieces of their unprecedented music aren't necessary.'

Led Zeppelin's fans, of course, did find its music necessary, and the album was number 1 for two weeks in the US. Without a tour to back it or a single release, however, it had the shortest chart life – 30 weeks – of any of the Zeppelin albums released during the band's existence.

'I think PRESENCE was a highly underrated record,' said Page. 'PRESENCE was pure anxiety and emotion. I mean, we didn't know if we'd ever be able to play in the same way again. It might have been a very dramatic change, if the worst had happened to Robert. PRESENCE is our best in terms of uninterrupted emotion.'

Left: **Led Zeppelin's concerts were characterized by lots of smoke and dramatic lighting effects, especially during Jimmy Page's violin bow guitar solos.**

Right: **Robert Plant on the move, John Bonham at rest.**

Below: **Jimmy Page onstage at the Los Angeles Forum, March 24, 1975.**

Below right: **Jimmy Page in a rare moment without a guitar in his hands.**

Left: ***Robert Plant and Jimmy Page at the New York premiere of*** **The Song Remains The Same,** ***Cinema One, October 20, 1976.***

Right: ***John Bonham behind his drum set during Led Zeppelin's final US tour in the summer of 1977.***

Below: ***Robert Plant and Jimmy Page on the 'Return to the Clubs' tour of England, March, 1971.***

Page returned to work on the concert film, and the double album SOUNDTRACK FROM THE FILM THE SONG REMAINS THE SAME *was released September 28, 1976, with the world premiere of the two hour 17 minute film on October 20. In interviews, Page was less than wildly enthusiastic about it. 'For a time, the movie was shelved,' he revealed, 'and we were going to come over here [the US] . . . and do some more footage. But after Robert's accident, we were forced to tie it all up. We'd done work with it already and it had to come out.'*

*'*THE SONG REMAINS THE SAME *was a live album,' Page said of the accompanying record, 'but it wasn't the best performance, it was just the one that happened to have celluloid with it.' In 1990, when Page was compiling the Led Zeppelin box set, it was not included in the retrospective.*

The film was an odd mixture of concert footage, fantasy sequences, and documentary filmmaking. The group's fantasies, which leaned heavily toward Arthurian legend (with the exception of Bonham's footage of farm life and drag racing), were predictable and a little silly. The movie's reviews were mostly negative, the worst coming from Dave Marsh in Rolling Stone, *who used it as an excuse to bury the group. 'It is hard to imagine another rock act making a film so guileless and*

revealing,' he wrote. 'Far from a monument to Zeppelin's stardom, THE SONG REMAINS THE SAME *is a tribute to their rapaciousness and inconsideration. While Led Zeppelin's music remains worthy of respect (even if their best songs are behind them) their sense of themselves merits only contempt.' Manager Peter Grant may have come close to the mark when he called the film 'the most expensive home movie ever made,' but film critic Leonard Maltin sums up general opinion best in the review in his* TV Movies & Video Guide Book, *awarding the film two stars and dubbing it 'for fans only.'*

Nevertheless, it remains a historical document revealing something of what a Led Zeppelin concert performance was like, with Page pulling screaming leads out of his Gibson, and Plant, his tight jeans hugging his hips, screeching out his high-pitched and high-decibel vocals. The standout is naturally STAIRWAY TO HEAVEN, *as Plant attempts to explicate the mystical lyrics with asides. 'I think this is a song of hope,' he notes at the outset (the 'I think' didn't make it on to the record). After singing, 'And the forests will echo with laughter,' he asks, 'Does anybody remember laughter?' then declares, 'But I've got some good news.' (In a spring 1991 interview in* Masters of Rock *magazine – an issue devoted to Led Zeppelin – Plant cited both* STAIRWAY TO HEAVEN*'s lyrical obscurity and message of hope as part of its appeal. 'I just think the ambiguity of the lyrics,' he said, in answer to Dia Stein's question. 'Everybody can interpret [the lyrics] however they will,' Plant continued. 'It's potential optimism, lyrically. It's saying that if you hold tight, you can make it all right.')*

The album is likewise a historical item. Even if it is not, as Page says, the best live Zeppelin, it does not seem unrepresentative of the band's live sound at a time when it was perhaps the top concert attraction in the US, if not the world. But film and record remain essentially curios in the Led Zeppelin catalog, stepchildren half-disowned by their parents and their audience. (Meanwhile, the business in bootlegged Zeppelin live recordings is so extensive that, by 1990, Robert Godwin's book The Illustrated Collector's Guide to Led Zeppelin *had run to a third edition of 480 pages, much of it given over to a list of bootlegs.)*

With the film out of the way, the band began rehearsing for its first American tour in two years, set to start in February 1977. Unfortunately, Plant developed tonsilitis, and the tour was pushed back, finally opening April 1 at the Dallas Memorial Auditorium. It continued, with breaks, into June, and included six sold-out concerts at Madison Square Garden. It was scheduled to continue into August, but the last date turned out to be a show at the Oakland Coliseum on July 24, a stop on the tour that also featured an altercation between the band and members of promoter Bill Graham's security force.

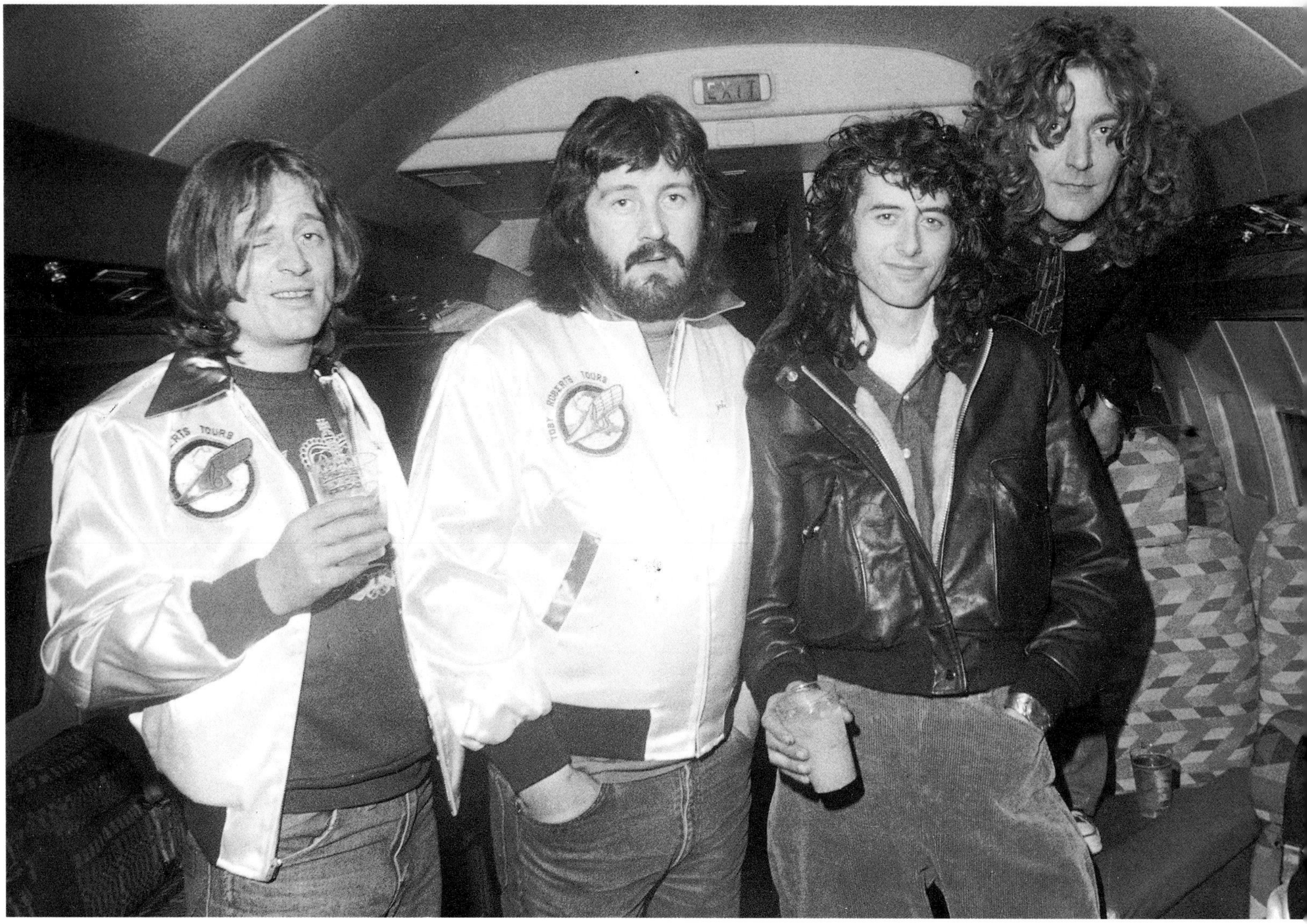
EXIT
TOBY ROBERTS TOURS

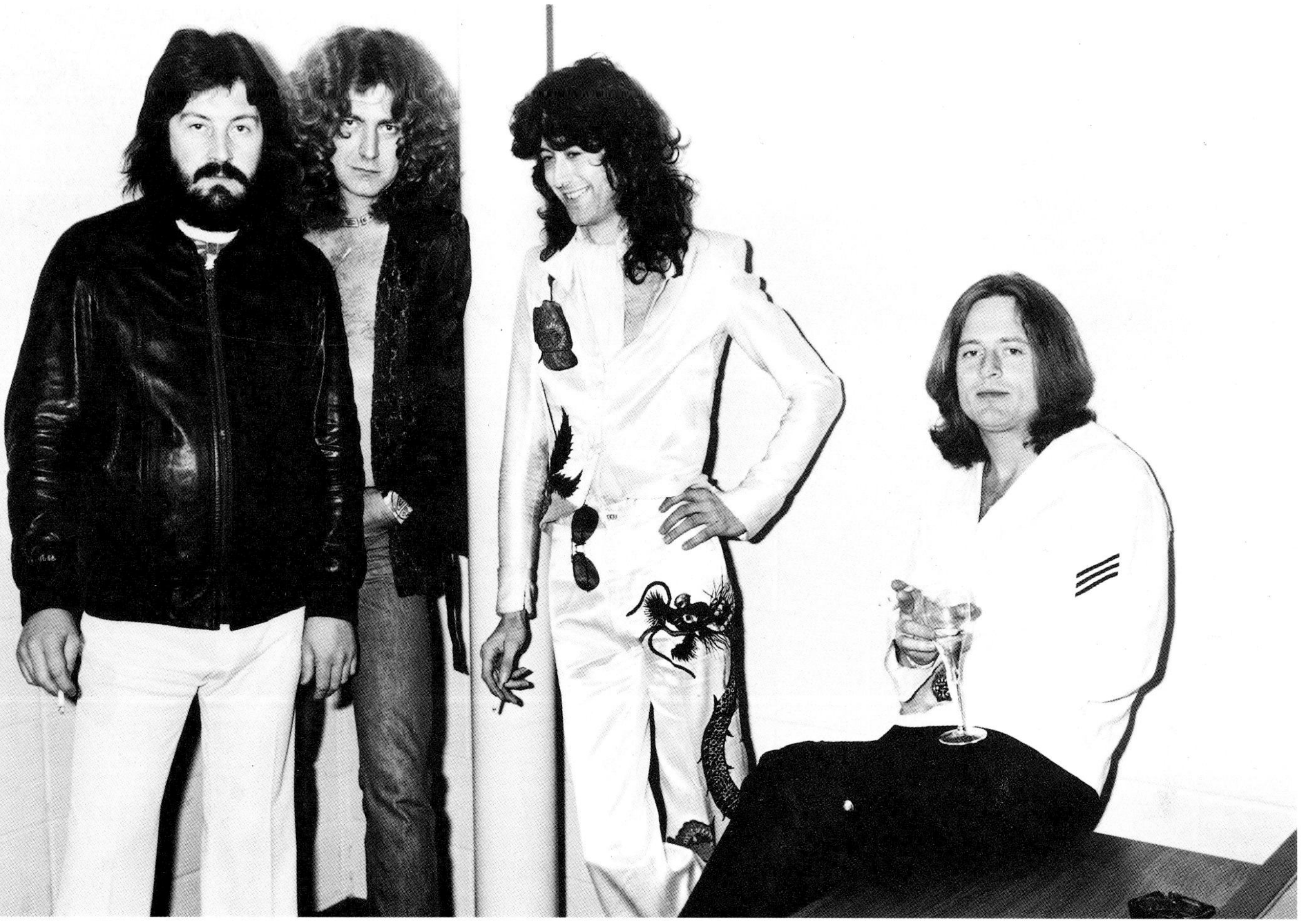

Above: **Led Zeppelin on their plane during the 1977 US tour.**

Previous pages: **Jimmy Page onstage at the Silverdome in Detroit, Michigan, April 30, 1977.**

Left: **Led Zeppelin relax before going onstage at the Silverdome in Detroit, Michigan, April 30, 1977.**

Above right: **John Paul Jones, Led Zeppelin's least prominent member, plays bass during the 1977 tour.**

Right: **Page and Plant visit a British radio station around the time of the release of the Led Zeppelin album In Through The Out Door in 1979.**

Left: **Jimmy Page onstage in San Diego, California, May 28, 1973. Note that John Bonham's bass drum displays his chosen symbol from the untitled Led Zeppelin album.**

Above: **Robert Plant onstage at Kezar Stadium, San Francisco, June 2, 1973.**

On July 27, Robert Plant's young son Karac died of a stomach ailment while his father was in the US, once again plunging the band into a state of uncertainty. The final 10 dates of the tour were canceled, and Plant rushed home. Led Zeppelin remained inactive for a long time, while rumors of a breakup circulated along with a sense that the group had become uniquely star-crossed.

Page gave a series of interviews in October 1977, in order to crush the rumors, and meanwhile he revealed plans for a live album that would contain a chronological sequence of recordings dating back to Led Zeppelin's 1969 performance at the Royal Albert Hall in London. To date, no such album has been released.

Led Zeppelin regrouped for rehearsals in May 1978, and Plant began turning up onstage with local bands and such performers as Swan Song's Dave Edmunds. In October, Jones and Bonham played on sessions for Paul McCartney's next Wings album. But it wasn't until late in the year that the group seriously got down to work on a new album, this time recorded

Below: **Led Zeppelin's final three '70s albums. Clockwise from top: In Through The Out Door *(1979)* with its brown paper sleeve; The Song Remains The Same *(1976)*; and Presence *(1976)*.**

at ABBA's Polar Studios in Stockholm. The album was finished by February, and Zeppelin prepared to return to the concert stage for a special occasion – the massive Knebworth Festival – in August 1979. The two memorable shows turned out to be the group's last ever in Great Britain.

IN THROUGH THE OUT DOOR, the new album, was released on August 15, 1979, and spent seven weeks at number 1 in the US, with FOOL IN THE RAIN hitting number 21 on the singles chart. At the same time, all eight of the band's previous Lps re-entered the charts.

Though it would turn out to be Led Zeppelin's final new studio release, IN THROUGH THE OUT DOOR is more suggestive of new directions for the band than any real conclusion to its work. If IN THE EVENING, the lead-off track, is reminiscent of the KASHMIR side of Zeppelin already familiar from PHYSICAL GRAFFITI and PRESENCE, SOUTH BOUND SUAREZ, with its rollicking piano, sounds like nothing the band had attempted before, while FOOL IN THE RAIN boasts a changing Latin American rhythm also new to the Zeppelin sound, and ALL MY LOVE sounds like a precursor to Robert Plant's solo albums.

'On this album,' wrote Howard Mylett in his book Jimmy Page: Tangents Within a Framework *(Mylett is also the author of a book on the whole group), 'Jimmy seemed to restrict his leads to points of emphasis on CAROUSELAMBRA where the song is sustained by the rhythm of keyboards. In fact John Paul Jones has at least as many solos and leads as Jimmy does on the album. Within the keyboards-oriented framework Jimmy cuts loose to a bracing effect and the variety on the album is particularly impressive.' 'It wasn't the most comfortable album,' said Page himself. 'I think it was very transitional . . . a springboard for what could have been.'*

Reviews were generally favorable, but unexcited, with some critics noting Zeppelin's total lack of response to the currently fashionable punk/new wave. (In fact, Plant and Page had been among the very few 'dinosaur' rock stars to listen to punk music, even venturing to punk clubs. And WEARING AND TEARING, an out-take from IN THROUGH THE OUT DOOR that finally turned up on CODA, indicated they had felt the new music's influence.) In general, however, the band was taken for granted on this release. 'Lax in the lyric department, as usual,' wrote Robert Christgau, 'but their best since HOUSES OF THE HOLY.' British critic Nick Kent noted, '[T]he band has never played better and it only remains to get the band back on the road and into a period of intense activity.'

Above: ***November 28, 1979, John Paul Jones, Robert Plant, and John Bonham attend the*** **Melody Maker** ***awards ceremony at the Waldorf Hotel in London, collecting awards for best live act, best band, best album, best guitarist, best producer, best composer, and best male singer.***

Right: ***Jimmy Page at the Silverdome, Detroit, Michigan, on April 30, 1977, where Led Zeppelin played before 76,229 people, breaking the attendance record they themselves had set.***

Above left: **John Bonham, perhaps rock's heaviest drummer, in action.**

Left: **Led Zeppelin backstage at the Knebworth Festival, August 4, 1979.**

Above: **John Bonham in what appears to be a quieter mood.**

But 'intense activity' was a thing of the past for Led Zeppelin. On December 29, Plant, Jones, and Bonham turned up for Paul McCartney's Kampuchea benefit at the Hammersmith Odeon in London, with Plant fronting Rockpile (a band featuring Dave Edmunds and new waver Nick Lowe) in a version of the Elvis Presley hit LITTLE SISTER, *and Jones and Bonham recreating their parts in McCartney's* ROCKESTRA THEME, *which had appeared on Wings'* BACK TO THE EGG *album. (Excerpts from the appearances were featured on the double Lp* CONCERTS FOR THE PEOPLE OF KAMPUCHEA *in 1981.)*

Led Zeppelin returned to concert activity on June 17, 1980, in Dortmund, Wastfelenhalle, West Germany, the start of a 14-date, three-week tour of relatively small halls in Europe that had to be considered a shakedown cruise for a more extensive trek. The tour ran through July 7, after which the group prepared for a North American tour, set to begin October 17 in Montreal. 'Over all, everyone has been dead chuffed with the way this tour's gone,' reported John Bonham. 'There were so many things that could have gone wrong. It was a bit of a gamble, this one, but it's worked really well.' It was one of his last public remarks.

On September 25, Bonham died at Jimmy Page's house after a rehearsal, the cause of death being accidental suffocation on vomit after a long bout of drinking.

There followed months of speculation about what the band would do, with the names of many drummers mentioned to replace Bonham. But on December 4, 1980, Led Zeppelin released a short statement: 'The loss of our dear friend, and the deep respect we have for his family . . . have led us to decide that we could not continue as we were.'

That didn't end speculation, but in late 1981, Page gave an interview to International Musician *magazine in which he elaborated on Led Zeppelin's future. 'Obviously, I really want to get out and play,' he said. 'I'd like to get a vehicle, a group of guys who will provide a vehicle for that, and that's the new project, sometime in the New Year. It'll need some time to get together, because I don't want to do anything that isn't one hundred percent terrific. It would be silly to even think about going on with Zeppelin. It would have been a total insult to John. I couldn't have played the numbers and looked round and seen someone else on the drums. It wouldn't have been an honest thing to do. No, it'll be new ideas, new material, and I'm dying to do it.' But it would take Page longer than he expected to find a new vehicle, and he wasn't through with Led Zeppelin yet, either.*

Left: ***Jimmy Page and Robert Plant, Zeppelin's principal songwriters, display their onstage camaraderie at the Silverdome in Detroit, April 30, 1977.***

Above: ***A publicity photo taken prior to the Knebworth Festival in August, 1979, shows Zeppelin's new 'New Wave' look: ties, pleated pants and sports jackets.***

CHAPTER FIVE

Coda

1981-1991

In 1981, Robert Plant began to gig around his home in a band called the Honeydrippers, while Jimmy Page worked on the soundtrack to the film DEATH WISH II, and John Paul Jones retired, resurfacing in 1985 with his own soundtrack album, for the film SCREAM FOR HELP. The DEATH WISH II soundtrack was released in early 1982 and featured several vocal tracks by Chris Farlowe, with whom Page had worked at Immediate Records during his session days. It reached number 40 in the UK and number 50 in the US.

Robert Plant, hooking up with guitarist Robbie Blunt, bassist Paul Martinez, and keyboard player Jess Woodroofe (and with Phil Collins and Cozy Powell sharing drumming duties), launched his solo career in June 1982, with his debut album, PICTURES AT ELEVEN, which reached number 5, went gold, and produced two minor hit singles in BURNING DOWN ONE SIDE and PLEDGE PIN. (In December 1990, PICTURES AT ELEVEN went platinum.)

In December 1982, Swan Song issued a posthumous Led Zeppelin album, CODA, consisting of out-takes from 1969 to 1978 and produced by Jimmy Page. Critically dismissed, it nevertheless reached number 6 in the US and number 4 in the UK, demonstrating Zeppelin's continuing appeal.

Plant returned with a second solo album, THE PRINCIPLE OF MOMENTS, in July 1983, and saw it reach number 8 and go platinum, producing the Top 40 hits BIG LOG and IN THE MOOD. Page returned to performing in September 1983, at Ronnie Lane's ARMS benefit for multiple sclerosis in London, where he played an instrumental version of STAIRWAY TO HEAVEN. He was featured on the subsequent set of US dates as well.

Page also accompanied Plant on the singer's biggest post-Zeppelin success the following year, with the release of the Ep THE HONEYDRIPPERS VOLUME ONE, on which Plant recreated fifties songs along with a backing that also included Jeff Beck and Nile Rodgers. The record reached number 4, with the single SEA OF LOVE hitting number 3, and a second single, ROCKIN' AT MIDNIGHT' getting to number 25 in 1985.

By this time Page finally had organized his first post-Zeppelin group, and the debut album by the Firm – Page, former Free and Bad Company vocalist Paul Rodgers, bassist Tony Franklin, and drummer Chris Slade – was released in February 1985. It reached number 17 and went gold, producing the number 28 single RADIOACTIVE and the number 78 SATISFACTION GUARANTEED. (Also released around this time was WHATEVER HAPPENED TO JUGULA?, Page's duo album with Roy Harper, which got to number 44 in the UK and did not chart in the US.)

Robert Plant suffered disappointment with his third solo album, SHAKEN 'N STIRRED, released in May 1985. The album got only to number 20 and a gold certification, with the single LITTLE BY LITTLE only reaching number 36.

On July 13, 1985, at JFK Stadium in Philadelphia, Led Zeppelin staged a reunion at the Live Aid concert. Page, Plant, and Jones, joined by Paul Martinez on keyboards and Phil Collins and Tony Thompson on drums, played ROCK AND ROLL, WHOLE LOTTA LOVE, and STAIRWAY TO HEAVEN to an audience as enraptured as ever at their sound.

In January 1986, Led Zeppelin, with Thompson on drums, held rehearsals in England for an intended reunion. But the group decided not to continue, and once again the former bandmembers went their separate ways. Page's Firm released its second album, MEAN BUSINESS, in February. With a minor hit single, ALL THE KINGS HORSES, the album got to number 22, but it was the band's final effort.

Right: **Jimmy Page at the Ronnie Lane benefit in 1983. He played an instrumental version of 'Stairway To Heaven.'**

Above: **Phil Collins and Robert Plant on Plant's first solo tour, September 12, 1983.**

Below: **Zeppelin's two posthumous albums,** Coda **(1982) and the** Led Zeppelin **boxed set (1990) compiled by Jimmy Page.**

Below: **The newly coiffed Robert Plant in his early solo days.**

Plant jettisoned his old band in 1987 and organized a new one. 'There was anxiety, anger, and frustration,' he said. 'Personnel-wise it wasn't happening any more; a kind of complacency had set in. When the tour finally ground to a halt, I knew I had to regroup.' The new band, led by guitarist Doug Boyle and keyboard player Phil Johnstone, recorded NOW AND ZEN, Plant's fourth solo album, released in March 1988 it rocked harder than previous efforts and the song TALL COOL ONE, reached number 25 on the singles chart and featured a guitar solo by Jimmy Page. Plant promoted the album heavily, agreeing to interviews in which he discussed his debt to Zeppelin. The return to an earlier style had the desired effect: NOW AND ZEN went platinum.

On May 14, 1988, another Led Zeppelin reunion took place at Madison Square Garden at the Atlantic Records 40th anniversary party, where Jason Bonham, John's son, played drums, and the group played WHOLE LOTTA LOVE and STAIRWAY TO HEAVEN. It was well-received, but speaking in April, 1991, manager Peter Grant said the two reunions Led Zeppelin had done had 'been disasters. Atlantic was dreadful.'

Above: ***Jimmy Page on tour with his post-Zeppelin band the Firm, promoting the band's debut album, in 1985. A versatile player, he switched from his usual Gibson Les Paul to the rival Fender Telecaster guitar.***

Right: ***Robert Plant onstage in Japan. Here he is accompanied by Pete Townshend of the Who (far right).***

Above: ***Robert Plant and Jimmy Page at Live Aid. John Paul Jones faces away at left.***

Right: ***Robert Plant onstage at Live Aid, JFK Stadium, Philadelphia, July 13, 1985.***

In July, Jimmy Page released his debut solo album, OUTRIDER, *with vocals by Plant, Chris Farlowe, and John Miles. The album reached number 26 and went gold.*

Robert Plant released his fifth solo album, MANIC NIRVANA, *in March, 1990. The album entered the Billboard chart on April 7 at number 39, and peaked at number 13 on April 28. It remained in the charts through September 22, its 25th week listed. It has been certified gold, and is said by Atlantic to be near platinum.*

Led Zeppelin staged two quasi-reunions in 1990. The band played at Jason Bonham's wedding in the spring, and Page joined Plant on stage for three songs at the Knebworth Festival in the UK in June, with the results released on KNEBWORTH: THE ALBUM *later in the summer. Plant's* MANIC NIRVANA *tour, after playing Europe, spent July and August in the US, concluding August 14 in Sacramento, California.*

Below left: **Robert Plant and Jimmy Page, a whole lotta love, at Live Aid.**

Below: **Robert Plant's second solo band. From left: Doug Boyle, Phil Johnstone, Plant, Chris Blackwell, Charlie Jones.**

Page, meanwhile, had been in Sterling Sound in New York the previous May, resequencing and digitally remastering tracks from the Led Zeppelin catalog for a massive box set retrospective. LED ZEPPELIN, *the four-CD set, was released in October 1990. (A two-CD version,* REMASTERS, *came out in England.) Running more than four and a half hours, the set was for all intents and purposes a slightly edited, resequenced version of the entire Zeppelin oeuvre. It contained two-thirds of the band's previously released material.*

Garnering favorable reviews, LED ZEPPELIN *became one of the most successful in the string of box set retrospectives that had been kicked off by Bob Dylan's* BIOGRAPH *in 1985 and continued by Eric Clapton's* CROSSROADS *in 1988. Outdistancing such competition as boxes by the Byrds, the Electric Light Orchestra, Elton John, and Frank Sinatra,* LED ZEPPELIN, *with a list price of almost $55, was the highest debuting release on the* Billboard *magazine album chart for the week ending November 10, 1990, at number 40. It peaked at number 18 the following week, went platinum in December, and stayed in the Top 200 for 19 weeks, until March 16, 1991.*

Rumors persist of a permanent Led Zeppelin reunion. In his April 1991 interview with Musician *magazine, band manager Peter Grant was asked if there were contingency plans ready in case Zeppelin decided to tour in 1991. 'I know that various promoters have it worked out,' Grant replied. 'I get calls constantly. But whether they'll ever do it, I don't know. Robert doesn't want to.'*

But the statement was hardly Sherman-like. Dire Straits manager Ed Bicknell, observed, 'Their strength is in North America. I know that in the conversations between them they've set aside – if they are going to do it at all – July to October of 1991. . . . I don't think they'd do Europe or the Far East.' 'They'd play North America,' said Grant, 'the UK, possibly Rio.' But even if such a thing should happen, Grant added, 'To me, personally, it could never be the same. It just couldn't.'

Below: **Robert Plant emotes at the Atlantic Records 40th anniversary, May 14, 1988, Madison Square Garden.**

Right: **Jimmy Page used his double-necked guitar for other songs besides 'Stairway To Heaven,' for example, employing it on the Firm's 1985 hit single 'Radioactive.'**

THE ORIGINAL SOUNDTRACK · MUSIC BY JIMMY PAGE
DEATH WISH II
JIMMY PAGE
OUTRIDER
MEAN BUSINESS
THE FIRM

ROBERT PLANT
NOW AND ZEN
robert plant
the principle of moments
robert plant
robert plant
the honey drippers
VOLUME ONE

The third quarter of 1991 came and went without a Led Zeppelin reunion, but there seems no reason why it shouldn't happen at some point. First, unlike other bands that have broken up, the members of Zeppelin do not seem to be suffering from business or personal disagreements, as their frequent reformings and tendencies to turn up on each other's recordings attest. Robert Plant's apparent reluctance may be due simply to concern for his ongoing, moderately successful solo career, but others have put aside moderate success for massive success before. And the final ingredient necessary to any reunion has never been in doubt: there is popular interest in having it take place. In fact, with the proliferation of clone bands and the continuing impact of the music, it's hard to think that popular demand for Led Zeppelin has diminished one iota in 10 years. This is not just a band that has stood the test of time; it's a group that defined its time and continues to set a standard for rock music today.

Above, far left: ***Jimmy Page's post-Zeppelin albums. Clockwise from top:*** **Death Wish II** ***(1982),*** **Outrider** ***(1988),*** **The Firm** ***(1985),*** **Mean Business** ***(1986).***

Above left: ***Robert Plant's post-Zeppelin albums. Clockwise from top:*** **The Principle Of Moments** ***(1983),*** **Shaken 'N Stirred** ***(1985),*** **The Honeydrippers Volume One** ***(1984),*** **Pictures At Eleven** ***(1982),*** **Now And Zen** ***(1988). Center:*** **Manic Nirvana** ***(1990).***

Above: ***Publicity photo of Jimmy Page issued upon the release of his debut solo album,*** **Outrider,** ***in 1988.***

Left: ***Robert Plant and Jimmy Page onstage at Madison Square Garden at the Atlantic Records 40th anniversary concert, May 14, 1988.***

Right: ***Publicity photo of Robert Plant issued upon the release of*** **Manic Nirvana.**

Discography

Led Zeppelin U.S. Discography

ALBUMS

Atlantic Led Zeppelin 1969
Atlantic Led Zeppelin II 1969
Atlantic Led Zeppelin III 1970
Atlantic [untitled] 1971
Atlantic Houses Of The Holy 1973
Swan Song Physical Graffiti 1975
Swan Song Presence 1976
Swan Song Soundtrack From The Film The Song Remains The Same 1976
Swan Song In Through The Out Door 1979
Swan Song Coda 1982
Atlantic Led Zeppelin 1990

SINGLES

Atlantic Good Times Bad Times/Communication Breakdown 1969
Atlantic Whole Lotta Love/Living, Loving Maid (She's Just A Woman) 1969
Atlantic The Immigrant Song/Hey Hey Can I Do 1970
Atlantic Black Dog/Misty Mountain Hop 1971
Atlantic Rock And Roll/Four Sticks 1971
Atlantic Over The Hills And Far Away/Dancing Days 1973
Atlantic D'yer Mak'er/The Crunge 1973
Swan Song Trampled Under Foot/Black Country Woman 1975
Swan Song Candy Store Rock/Royal Orleans 1976
Swan Song Fool In The Rain/Hot Dog 1979

Jimmy Page U.S. Albums Discography

[Note: From 1964 to 1966, Jimmy Page participated in numerous studio sessions as a hired musician. He was a member of the Yardbirds from 1966 to 1968, of Led Zeppelin from 1968 to 1980, and of the Firm from 1985 to 1986. He sometimes did session work while in these groups. Only his post-Led Zeppelin work is listed here.]

Swan Song Death Wish II: Original Motion Picture Soundtrack 1982
Atlantic The Firm 1985
Atlantic Mean Business: The Firm 1986
Geffen Outrider 1988

John Paul Jones U.S. Albums Discography

[Note: From 1964 to 1968, John Paul Jones participated in numerous studio sessions as a hired musician. He was a member of Led Zeppeliln from 1968 to 1980. He sometimes did session work while in the group. Only his post-Led Zeppelin work is noted here.]

Atlantic Scream For Help: Original Motion Picture Soundtrack 1985

Robert Plant U.S. Albums Discography

Swan Song Pictures At Eleven 1982
Es Paranza The Principle Of Moments 1983
Es Paranza The Honeydrippers Volume One 1984
Es Paranza Shaken 'N Stirred 1985
Es Paranza Now And Zen 1988
Es Paranza Manic Nirvana 1990

Index

Acknowledgments

The publisher would like to thank Adrian Hodgkins the designer, Sara Dunphy for picture research, Helen Dawson for preparing the index and the agencies and individuals listed below for supplying the photographs:

Bettmann Archive: pages 28 top, 36 bottom, 37, 60 right, 76 bottom
BPL pages 4, 12, 17 top, 21 left, 22 top, 25 top, 30, 44, 64, 65, 73, 77 top and bottom
Chris Fallo: pages 8 top, 32, 46 bottom, 60 left, 70, 74, 76 top two
Galella: pages 68 top, 72 both
Globe: pages 1, 7, 13 both, 15, 19 bottom, 20 top and bottom, 21 right, 24, 25 right and bottom left, 27, 38 both, 41, 49, 51 top, 53, 56 bottom, 59, 61
Photofeatures International: page 9 bottom, 18, 39, 40 top, 48 top, 50, 51 bottom left, 52 both, 55, 58, 62 bottom
Photofest: page 56 top
Pictorial Press: pages 2-3, 9 top, 10, 11, 16, 17 bottom, 18 top, 19 top, 22 bottom, 27 top, 28 bottom, 29, 31, 33, 36 top, 43, 45 top and bottom, 47, 48 bottom, 51 bottom right, 57 bottom, 62 top, 63
Rangefinders: page 75
Relay Photos: page 57 top
Rex Photos: pages 8 bottom, 23, 26, 35, 67, 69, 71, 79